LIFE IS WORTH MORE THAN JUST LIVING

Waking up with a Purpose and not an Agenda

Grace C. Okoro

LIFE IS WORTH MORE THAN JUST LIVING

Copyright © 2021

Written by Grace C. Okoro

Edited by Samantha Belson – sbelson@twu.edu

Cover Design & Formatting by ArashJahani.com

Paperback ISBN: 978-0-578-34693-9

Acknowledgement

This book is dedicated to everyone who believes that there is more to life than just meets the eye. I dedicate this book to my family and friends who believe and support me in all I do. My parents who supported me in a time where I could not support myself, I say thank you. To my siblings who always reminded me that I could do anything I put my mind to, I say thank you. To my church family, for all your prayers and well wishes, I say thank you. To God who instilled in me the wisdom and understanding needed to believe that all things are possible, I say thank you. For I am who I am by your grace, love, and mercy.

Contents

Contents

Note to Self

There are people in this world who look up to you. There are young girls and boys that see you as beautiful, successful, and a great woman after God's own heart. Stop looking for affection and attention from people who look down on you and only care about their own selfish agenda. Do it for the ones who are proud of you, look up to you, and want to see you win. There are people that admire you, so stop comparing and trying to be like others. Be yourself. Be the best you can be because to many you will be an example of Gods light. God has set you apart to do great things, so don't fear, he has already given you everything you need to succeed. Be grateful for the things you have now so that when God gives you more, you will be able to handle it with grace. Wanting to be the best you can be is good, but don't let that desire consume you. Grow with grace and humility. Remember God loves you; he cares for you, and wants you to succeed. Don't forget him when you reach the top.

Chapter 1

The Journey Begins

Growing up, I never knew exactly what I wanted to be; I just knew it would be something great. My mother wanted me to be a nurse, and hoped my siblings would study something in the medical field as well. My mother worked in a major hospital in Houston, and as any African parent, she and my father believed that success came from going to school and getting a high-paying job. I don't believe many parents know what a "high paying" job really is, but if your job pays the bills, gives you nice clothes, a nice home, and enough money to pay your tithes at church, it was a job worth getting. To me, I never wanted to be a nurse, but I was young so I went along with it. As I grew up, I still wasn't sure what I wanted to do, but I knew it was going to be something astonishing. I saw many of my family members who worked in the medical field always complaining and looking stressed out, but for some reason were still telling their children to follow in their footsteps. I could never understand why, but I knew that wasn't going to be me. It wasn't until I got older that I realized people live in generational cycles that can only stop if someone decides to jump off, and I was willing to jump off. We live in a world where everyone wants to belong, and in order to belong you have to feel accepted no matter how miserable you are. I soon learned that everyone had their own version of reality, and a limited one at that. I always believed that nothing in life was impossible to achieve, but when I would speak to some of my family members and friends about one day becoming a millionaire, they laughed at the thought.

To them, becoming a millionaire was impossible, but to me making money seemed as easy as getting a glass of water from the sink faucet. I soon realized that my mindset on how I perceived the world was different than their own. I realized that it was never that I hated nursing, or that I thought myself to be above it, but it reminded me of a life I did not want. Every time I would see a nurse, they never seemed happy, always looked stressed, and seemed miserable. I correlated that to the field itself and not the fact that maybe the nurses I saw just hated their jobs, or went into a field that was not favorable to them. It started to dawn on me that many people are in careers they hate because they are following another person's vision for their life and not their own. It is possible that if I did nursing I would have been happy—or maybe I would be miserable–but one thing is for sure, I followed the vision and plan God set out for me, and I can say I love what God has me doing now. Why certain individuals can look at making millions of dollars as something impossible is because they have no vision. Like Sarah from the bible, they live in what they believe to be real, and not in the possibility of the unknown. Sarah in the bible was told she would conceive a child, but at the time she was very old. I think "very old" is an understatement. Let me put it this way, conceiving at her age had never been done before. Although she did not believe it to be true, it still happened. Same with all those who believe that certain things can only happen to a certain type of people. The issue wasn't that it couldn't be done, the issue was that they never asked the right questions.

As a teenager, I never had any doubt that the life I dreamed of would come to be a reality. I always believed that in order for it to happen I had to first understand how millionaires were becoming millionaires. In trying to understand the how, I was then able to learn that it all begins in the mind, your way of thinking determines your outcome. It was then that a "high paying" job went from earning few thousand dollars a month to knowing that what an average person makes in a year could be made within the first fiscal quarter. I was now in the moneymaking business. My family and I love watching football, and I would hear some of the numbers some of these players were making, I couldn't believe it. I knew at that time I could never play football because I was not a guy, but what I realized from what I learned was that making such an amount was possible. I never fault the people in my life that doubted, or believed that my dreams were just that, a dream, because I knew their way of thinking was embedded in them by their environment and up-bringing. God knows why he tells us to "train a child in the way that he/she should go, so that when they are old they do not depart from those ways." Unfortunately, many people train their children to believe that there is only one way in life to achieve their goals, and if that way is not done, then they have failed. The unfortunate truth is that because of this, many children do indeed fail. Imagine if the only thing people could do in life was accounting, if you suck at math, well I guess that's it for you, life as you know it is over. That's the way some children are being raised. They believe that life is only one way, and once you've gotten off that course or track you are looked at as a failure before you have even failed.

I have had my struggles also with trying to please the world, my family, and people. At a point in time, I lost myself and was looking to people to tell me who I was. I was misled, deceived, and almost destroyed in the hands of people. I then knew that the only one who could tell me who I am is the one who created me, and that was God himself. It's funny how a person can look to another person to tell them who they are, when the person they are asking has no clue who they are themselves. It's like an individual who is known for having a bad odor telling another person which deodorant to use, or a broke professor who owes debt teaching a class full of students on how to manage finances. I don't know about you, but I want to follow someone who actually has proof that what they do or have done works. Many of us know that faith without works is dead, so I made sure that my faith was backed up with action. I knew I had no one in my life that I could talk to about making millions of dollars, and I was tired of hearing words that were discouraging so I took to the media, YouTube, and reality shows. Yes, *Keeping up with the Kardashians* was on my recorded shows list. I needed to see the world in a view that I had never seen before, and this family of 8 at the time showed me just that. I was able to see different places in the world because in the show the Kardashians traveled a lot, and I saw homes and a life that I never knew existed. For some people, where they are born or where they grow up is the only place they know, and to me that is sad. Even though the show allowed me to see life in a more expensive and glamorous way, I still needed to know how money worked, and how I would be able to make it.

YouTube is such an interesting place because it has almost everything you need on there. I watched videos on how to become an entrepreneur, how to make millions, how to think like a millionaire, and how to be a millionaire, but yet I was still broke. I filled myself with so much knowledge, and applied this knowledge in stocks and savings, but still, no millions. What was I doing wrong? I later realized I was doing everything by the books, and applying those things, but I lacked the influence and affluence needed to manifest these practices. Through people you gain connections, through connections you get opportunities, and like people say, "When opportunity meets preparation, you get success." For years, I chased greatness believing that greatness came through fame, riches, and power. It was not until recently that I discovered I can't chase what I already am. I realized that great dwells inside a person, it is not a trained skillset. You are great when you believe that there is more to life than the standards people set. You are great when every time you are told you can't, you get back up and try again, but with a newer and better strategy than before.

Thomas Edison was great because his perseverance and drive caused him to succeed. He could have given up after the first 30 failures like many people, but he believed that it was possible to create light through energy, and so he did. No one can learn greatness, it is something that is embedded in a person, through the belief that "What I am seeing can be done." The reason why people laughed at Thomas Edison, laughed at Noah who built the ark, and even laughed at Martin Luther King who had a dream was because they couldn't see the vision. God put in these people just as he puts in you and me, the visions and capacity needed to bring the dream to life. Some live big because they dream big, and some live small because they dream small. I can't possibly get you to understand what God put in me because if you could understand, he would have put it in you too. God looks for people who are willing to step out of what they believe to be ordinary so that he can fulfill his plan of extraordinary through them. If Thomas Edison came to me and said he wanted to create something that was never seen before, I would not understand it because the vision was not given to me, I could support him, yes, but even if I didn't it shouldn't stop him from continuing on with the vision.

The issue with people today is when they are given a vision, they look for people to co-sign on it or tell them how it will come into manifestation. You were given the dream or the vision, and you have all the blueprints to bring it into realization, just because others can't see it doesn't mean it is not true. Everything we have today was created by someone, who was laughed at by another. The airplanes we fly in are one. Who could have imagined that humans would be flying in the air like birds in the sky? I know it was a vision that seemed impossible to many, but to the ones the vision was given to, it was a possibility, that became a reality. The saying "many are called, but only a few are chosen," is the truth we live in because a lot of people reject all that God puts in them to do. People get ideas given to them by God, to create all that he places in their hearts to do, but after listening to naysayers, unbelievers, and people who have a limited mindset, they push those ideas aside. I always knew that the human mind if not protected could be easily influenced, that is why I made sure to use the bible as my blueprint in life. Noah's ark showed me that if we listen to people and not the voice of God then we, like everyone else, will get carried away with the storms of life. Thank God Noah decided to build that ark.

I've come to learn that there are two people in life: people who are living their dreams and people who are living their fears. If you wake up every day happy, you took that leap of faith and it worked out, then you know you are living your dream, but if you wake up seeing everyone else living and you start reminiscing on what you could have done or should have been, then you are living in your fears. I learned in my chase for fame that the plans God has for you is so much better than the plans you have for yourself. I could have had all the money, fame, and riches in the world, but what would it profit me if all those things destroyed me, and led me into drugs and addiction? It was then when I stopped fighting God's will that I began to understand what my purpose is, why I am alive, and what I am meant to do in the world. When I was at a stage in life where I was still figuring things out, I fell in love with writing music. I loved music because it was a platform in which my voice could be heard. I believed at that time that I would make music people could vibe to and grow from. I was comfortable with my newfound love for music that I thought surely, this is what God intends for me to do. I was moving in the right direction, just got off at the wrong stop. What I mean by this is my desire for writing was correct, but not in the area I believed it to be. Let me use a school bus as a representation of life. The goal of the bus is to drop children, which is us, home, but it is up to the children to know when to get off. The bus is going in the right direction, but if you get off one stop early, or one-stop late, you've missed your destination. The destination is your purpose. You can still get to your destination, but like those children who got off too early or too late, you now have to walk. Although time was wasted, the destination can still be reached. Either the parent, which is God, will come looking for the child, or the child will remember that this street is not my street; it's the next one. How could this incident be avoided? By asking the right questions. Asking the right questions can save you time and energy, and limit mistakes.

I had many missed routes and early stops, but God always came looking for me. I can admit the trial and error has not been fun, but as humans, we have our plans and God has his plans. Many feel that God will honor their plans because he grants the desires of one's heart, but the truth is that it is God putting the desires in our hearts, and through doing that he can help navigate us through life. I used to think rapping, fame, and money was my desire, but I realized that I desired to have a voice, a platform in which I would be heard, and money to establish it. I thought music was an easy route to get all these things at once, but God knew that my desire would be met, but in the way that would bring glory to his name. One might ask, "How would you know when something is not meant for you?" There are many signs that a person gets when something they want is not for them. One sign is you lack clarity. If you find yourself in a situation where you are always confused as to why this is happening or why that, you're most likely in something that isn't meant for you. Some other signs are unhappiness, built-up resentment, and exhaustion from always trying to make it work. Lastly, you ask yourself repeatedly if this is really what you are supposed to be doing. When you are in alignment with your purpose, there is peace. You can be yourself without feeling like who you are isn't good enough. In music, I was trying to fit who I was with a stage character that I created. I was trying to not lose myself or my identity in music, but found myself trying to appeal to a certain crowd. Then it dawned on me that, whether it is parents, culture, or the world, many people live their lives to please others, neglecting their true calling or identity. I wonder, can a person have true happiness in life, if the life they are living is not theirs to begin with? I'm not writing this to say not to listen to people because it is through people God can show himself true, but I am saying you have to be connected to the voice inside you, the voice I call the holy spirit because that voice is what is leading you to your purpose. For some life is being born, going to work, going to school, getting married, having kids, those kids having kids, then death. For me, life is being born for a purpose and that purpose is to inspire, motivate, uplift, create, and build. You can decide to live in the world, and be forgotten, or you can decide to help build it, and leave a lasting legacy: the choice is yours.

Chapter 2

Just A Little More Good

It is said that when you "do good, good things will happen to you." I wish life could be that easy. Many people in the world have done many questionable things, and things often go well for them, while for others, things seem to go bad. Is it that the ones who "do good" weren't so good after all? I often ask myself that question. Sometimes I wonder, am I not good enough? Maybe that's why I have struggles, or is the saying just a bunch of bull? I've had some time to think over this matter, and I am starting to believe that maybe in the areas we do good, we receive good, and in the areas we do bad, we receive bad. No one is perfect, and no one knows what a person does behind closed doors to say they are good, nor do we know the hearts of people to say they are bad. I find myself trying to do good, and good things have indeed happened to me. I also find myself doing bad, and let's just say Karma is real and working overtime. I believe the world is created to serve back what has been put out. I say this because lately, I have found myself struggling with so many things mentally due to the behaviors of others. I have asked myself, "What did I do to cause this, or am I facing the evil and jealousy of others?" I'm not sure anymore, but I have decided to live a life that is "good," whatever that means. All I can say is that my choices and actions will continue to reflect positivity and good towards others, and I will begin to surround myself with people who want such also. I have found myself being dragged into the reaction of someone else's actions, and although I have not done bad, my association with such a person has made me seem as though I have. In other words, your actions and the actions of the people around you can also affect your life. I have heard sad stories about "good" people's lives destroyed because of another person. I think it is true that good things happen to good people, I just now believe it is more complex than we think. Doing good is one thing, but that good won't matter if everyone around you is doing badly. Maybe the saying should be "do good and surround yourself with good, then good things will happen to you." I guess I'll have to try it to find out.

I had a discussion some time ago with one of my siblings, and in that discussion, I stated, a king doesn't have to make anyone believe he is king; he just has to be king. In other words, a person doesn't have to prove to people they are good, funny, kind, or great they just have to be themselves, and those things will show forth. At times, we find ourselves trying to prove our worth and greatness to the world instead of just letting it show through our character and actions. I used to struggle with this a lot. I would try so hard to show people that I am all these great things, but I later realized that maybe it's not them that needs to believe it; maybe, it's me. Like many of you, I faced a lot of insecurities, and those insecurities held me back from doing so much in life. I remember being told daily how beautiful I looked. Unfortunately, I had trouble seeing it, so I held on to the lies I believed were true about me. It always baffled me how five people could say I'm beautiful, but as soon as one person rejects me or is not attracted to me, I neglect the five voices and cling to that one. I guess the principle of majority rules was not a principle I followed. I realized that to feel approved, one needs to approve themselves first. It will be extremely difficult trying to prove to the world that you are something if you don't believe it yourself. Can you imagine a math teacher teaching students how to solve a problem he can't seem to solve himself? If the question is 5 + 5 and everyone gets 9, well, I guess the answer would just have to be 9. That's how many people are living life. They are not sure of who they are, so they look to the world to confirm it for them.

No one can tell you who you are because no one knows the gifts and talents God has put inside you. If I was to tell anyone as a child that I would be who I am now, they probably would have laughed or given an encouraging response, they themselves didn't believe. Loving yourself and putting yourself first does not make you selfish or self-centered. People confuse being selfish and only caring about yourself with putting yourself first. These are two separate things. One does not come from a place of love, while the other is the understanding that if I cannot love myself, then I cannot love you. Once I truly started loving myself, I understood what I was worth, and what I deserved from life and people. There is nothing in life that is impossible. Don't limit yourself to the sky when people have gone to the moon. You can decide to be your worst enemy by never believing in yourself and your strengths, or you can be an example to the world that nothing is unattainable. I am who I am today not by my power, but by the grace of God, and I am so glad that I was able to give up all I had planned and hoped for to follow the plans of God. In this world, we can blame others for the failures in our lives, or we can pick ourselves up and try again. This time we will be stronger because we are now aware of what caused us to fall and will not make that mistake again. Take heart and be encouraged. You are great, and you can do excellent things in this world, just remember to believe in yourself even if others do not.

I don't pride myself on being the best Christian. I know many people look up to me and want me to be this woman of God who makes no mistakes, doesn't get angry, and stays away from sin, but it gets lonely trying to do right when it feels like the world accepts everything wrong. I remember when I was younger; I was carefree and just liked the freedom of living. I wasn't worried about good or bad, right or wrong; I just went on this journey called life. What made me different was my love for God. I talked to God every day, and I don't mean the regular talk you do during prayers, but a full-on conversation. My relationship with God grew stronger and my life automatically started to change. Did I still get into trouble? Yes. Did I still struggle with sexual sins? Yes. But I was changing.

Fast-forward, now I'm in college. College was a time that was supposed to be fun, filled with experiences and relationships. Instead, my college experience was an experience filled with a struggle between right and wrong, good and bad. I wanted to be loved, and guys just weren't able to give me that love. To please them, I found myself displeasing God. It got to a point in life when I asked myself how long will I turn my back on God's love for men who cared less about me. It was tough because feeling alone is painful. I found peace with Christ for the most part, but the lack of physical affection weighed heavy on me. I have not made the best decisions or spoken in ways that people would call "Christian-like," but that was a role I never wanted to take. I was just a young girl who loved God, and God loved me back, and so my life changed. I'm happy that people look up to me as an example of what is good. I hope that as I journey through life, I don't let them down. I try so hard to ignore the pressure of being perfect because I know what it's like to feel imperfect, and I don't want my life to be all about fitting in. God has improved my life and is still perfecting it, and although people can see what God is doing for me on the outside, the pruning on the inside is what people can't see. What I would say to any young girl or guy reading this is, don't lose yourself in hopes to please people. Love yourself first, value your worth, and never settle to please anyone because you will be disappointed with yourself in the end.

Unfortunately, people like to make excuses for why their life ended up the way it did instead of taking ownership of the choices they made that caused the disappointment. When I was younger, I believed there was an explanation for everything that did or could happen — until now. People always find it easy to blame others for their failures but find it hard to blame themselves. Maybe it's pride or a belief that they are perfect. Whatever the reason may be, the question becomes this: "What are you going to do about it?" As people, we can decide to stop because every one of our efforts has failed us, or we can decide that we will not accept things the way they are and fight for the life we want. When I decided to write this book, I didn't have this topic in mind. I was frustrated at the outcome of certain decisions that I have made in my life. Maybe this ties into that, or maybe, God wanted me to write this because writing this will touch someone who might read it. Whatever the reason, I will just let it flow as it may.

These days I struggle with who I was and who I am now. I will admit I like this version of me a lot better than the one before, but it scares me. It scares me because I have no control over it. To those who might ask, "But why? We are the deciders of our destiny." My response to them is, "Are we?" If I had control over my life, I would be a rapper right now, married to a football player. It's not saying those things are impossible, but trying to achieve them didn't work out for me. I can decide to continue to pursue those things, but who will be at fault after years pass by, and it didn't come to fruition, or I achieve these things and realize there is no happiness. I guess I'll never know.

I always believed as a child that anything is possible if only you believe and go for it. God has a plan for us all, and if we are not aligning ourselves to that plan, life can become a struggle. There is so much more to life than we can understand. Maybe we don't understand it because we don't ask the right questions. Instead, we look for who to blame. I believe it's time to trust the process and listen to what life is telling us. There are three reasons why things don't work out for people in life.

1. It's not time
2. It's not meant for you
3. You are not ready to receive it yet

There are things in life that are not meant for us because if given to us, they can destroy us. There are things that are meant for us, we are just not ready to receive them yet. If God blessed you with a million dollars right now and you don't have any knowledge on how to save or invest, then after about a year a two you will find yourself broke again. I'm sure your mom needs a new house, and debts for you and all your loved ones need to be paid, and daddy needs a new car, and don't forget about the house and car for yourself. After being a financial savior to everyone and continuing to release money without any coming back in return, you will find out how quickly a million dollars can move. This is not to say, don't follow your dreams, this is just to say let us not look for who to blame if things don't work out. I pray that your heart's desires will be in alignment with God's will, and things will go well with you. In all things remember, take responsibility, don't blame others, and never give up on what you truly desire. For nothing is impossible.

Chapter 3

Hidden Pains

O ver the years, I have come across many different types of people. Some people pretend to be good but are bad, while others put up a wall due to past hurts, leading people to believe they are bad. Last month, I met a good guy in a lot of pain. Any kind and nurturing person would want to reach deep down inside his pain and pull him out, but I know that no one can truly do that. I can love him, give him my all, but will that be enough? Sometimes the truth is the person in pain needs to heal before they can let anyone in. Sometimes they need a friend to be there with them until they are ready to come out. The question is, Can you be that friend when you are hurting too? Pain comes in many unique forms, whether you lost a loved one, just faced divorce, a break up, or witnessed injustice, the pain from such a loss or experience is very painful. A broken heart is a metaphor for deep emotional pain. It is pain that takes time to heal if it ever heals at all. The question now is how do you heal a broken heart? Maybe there is no answer to that question.

Some may mutually agree that time does indeed heal a broken heart, but does it? A woman lost her father when she was 22 years old. Of course, the pain of her father's death was hard to bear, but as time passed on, she was able to accept what had happened. 8 years later, the young woman was standing in the dressing room at her wedding. The day that was supposed to be a joy for her, was not quite so. The fact that she was going to walk down the aisle without her father was hard for her to imagine. Time indeed gives a person the ability to heal or come to terms with what has happened, and for many people, time is the healing because they can go through life stronger and not emotionally affected by the thought. But, if time had healed her broken heart, then why at a moment such as her wedding was the pain of her dead father breaking her heart all over again? I guess one can say that there are levels to a broken heart, and the healing is dependent on the specific circumstance.

For instance, the pain of a broken heart from a relationship can heal more effectively than the pain from a death. This may be true, or pain tolerance could be dependent on the emotional or spiritual strength of a person. Someone who has hope that there is a better spouse or partner for them will heal faster than someone who believes that they cannot find better. Someone who believes that their loved one who has been suffering from cancer is now pain-free sitting with God in heaven has a better time in dealing with a broken heart than someone who believes that life ends here on earth. What I'm saying is there might not be a direct answer to what heals a broken heart, but one thing that I can say for sure is with time you become stronger if you are guided by hope and strengthened spiritually by God. The family of George Floyd is facing heartbreak at this time because their loved one was taken unjustly and cruelly. What makes their hearts painless is seeing the response of support from the world. This gives them hope knowing George's death will have an impact on the change to come for African Americans in the future. I pray for all the people in the world who have faced heartbreak, that they will find peace at this moment, knowing that "Pain may endure for a night, but joy cometh in the morning." Psalm 30:5

Chapter 4

The Relation(ships) of Life

Over the years, I've learned many things from all the relationships I encountered, but one thing I've learned for sure, is that God wants me to focus on him. When I focus on God, he allows me to receive all the great things he has planned for me. Since I was young, every relationship I have ever been in was because I initiated the first step, or had one of my friends link us together. As I got older, things started changing, and I wasn't having any luck getting a relationship. I was having more of a heartbreak-ship than a relationship. I say this because I was having the heartbreak of someone who was in a relationship without actually being in one. I realized that pursuing guys wasn't working for me, and I had to stop. I decided to stop going after guys I had feelings for, and trust completely in God to work everything out for me. God can see in people the things we cannot. For example, I may like a guy because to me through his presentation, he seems like a good guy, but God will help expose the things in his life that I would have not been able to see, until later in the relationship. We can see the outside of a person, but God sees the inside. Don't get me wrong, telling a guy how you feel is not a bad thing; no one should live in fear of rejection or hurt. However, one thing I've learned for sure is that guys know what they want, and if they don't pursue you, the relationship becomes one-sided.

When you go after a guy and you tell him how you feel without him expressing his love for you, the relationship then becomes all about you and how you feel about him. His heart will never truly be there because you never allowed it to be. He may really like you, but there is a chance that your love for him will be more than his love for you. It wasn't a mistake when God said, "A man that finds a wife, finds a good thing" (Proverbs 18:22). For me, this was hard to accept because I liked control, and felt like maybe the guy I like doesn't know I like him, or is intimidated, so if I let them know I'm interested and take the first step things will work out. I was very wrong. I noticed that many of the guys I pursued and fought so heavily for, were doing the same thing for another girl. So I was always left with the question: How come he never pursued me? Was it because I was making it so easy, or was I just not the girl they wanted? As I got closer to God, I realized that it was never my job to find a guy and prove to him that I am great, beautiful, or the one for him. If he believed that I was, he would ensure that I felt beautiful and great through his actions towards me.

In a relationship, you should be free to be yourself:

happy, in love, full of joy and laughter. Any relationship that makes you feel stressed, inadequate, and gives you the desire to want to impress, is not a relationship you want to be in. Don't listen to the lies of this world that say, "Love is blind." Love is many things, but it is not blind. Lust is what blinds you from seeing the truth. Spend your singleness loving God, traveling, and finding yourself. Guys really do know what they want, and if they don't pursue you, it's okay. Just keep living and inspiring, and a great guy who is meant for you will find you, I guarantee it. They say men go after what they want, and if a man does not come after you, he isn't that interested. So does that mean when you like a guy and he doesn't come after you, that he doesn't like you at all?

For years, I could never understand why the guys I liked would show interest but never approach me, while the guys I did not like would. I am a firm believer in never settling no matter the case, but as a single woman who one day would like to get married, does this mean I will have to give the guys I am not interested in a chance even though I know there is absolutely nothing there? I never thought I would be in the situation I am in now, because when I was younger dating wasn't an issue for me, so it left me to wonder what had changed. Was I better looking when I was younger than I am now, or is God trying to keep me single to show me something about relationships or myself? I was very superficial growing up; to me, it was all about looks. I believed there was such a thing as the "perfect guy." Now I am in a stage in life where looks still matter, of course, but looks are no longer my leading factor. I am not looking for the tallest, most handsome guy in the world that's perfect in all his ways, because I know people may have it all in one area but lack something in another. I just want a guy who I am attracted to, loves God dearly, and loves me unconditionally. I want him to love his family, and also love mine, to be caring, nice, hardworking, funny, faithful, and a joy to be around. I am not praying for some unrealistic guy that many women hope to find, because I know that life is a journey and we become better as time goes by. One thing is for sure, love is real, and it is made perfect with God. Being single can be tough at times, especially if you are ready to date, but one thing I have learned in my season of singleness is to stay firm. In this season is where you will find yourself, who you are, and who you want to become. Don't be afraid of giving people chances- there is no harm in going on dates and giving people you would not typically go for a chance, who knows you may fall in love. One thing remains the same, never settle or be in a situation with someone because you have no hope. Trust the process, in due time your love will come. I have gone through the process and it is painful but rewarding. It is rewarding because you become stronger, which helps you know what you want in a significant other, and how they are supposed to treat you.

I noticed a guy who I've known for a while, but never gave any attention to. He was sweet and caring and he made me feel beautiful. When I was around him, I felt like I was the only woman that mattered to him. To cut a long story short, he made me feel important, beautiful, and secure. Then something changed. Like always, the happiness I felt went away as the guy that brought me gladness became distant and uninterested. I don't know why that is. I am never the one to point blame on others, I like to look at myself first to check and see if I came on too strong or blunt, or if I was too distant and pushed them away. For once, I can say that it wasn't me. I am beautiful, strong, caring, and I was able to put away my selfish pride and put him first. I did not allow myself to retreat into my old patterns. I tried to be his friend, I reached out to him (not allowing my pride to get in the way of the fact that he never reached out to me first). I told myself pride doesn't get a person far, and a relationship is not a game of who reaches out first. I even gave him space so that he could find himself again. I know that he's not the one, because love is patient, it does not boast or brag, but most especially love does not hurt or leave you feeling like you are not enough. I am proud to know that I handled myself better this time. I was able to let go without destroying any friendship we had. Usually in the past, I would hurt the feelings of the guy that broke my heart because I was hurt, and I made it a goal to be the most beautiful person that would walk in the room so they could know what they lost. Now, I move on knowing that there is better. I move on knowing that I am enough, beautiful, and deserving of someone who will appreciate all of me.

The guy I am speaking of at the moment is actually a really great guy, and I mean that honestly. He is a good guy with a great heart that loves people, but he just can't love me the way I deserve to be loved. It's true, it may not be the right time for us, or it may never be, but one thing is for sure, I am better now than I was before! No one can say they are experts in relationships. When I watch relationship shows, I can tell they themselves are shocked if a relationship is continued outside the show. After many failed attempts at love, I stopped relying on looks and started relying solely on God. It was a struggle because I still was trying to control everything, and maybe didn't fully trust that God would bring me exactly what I liked. This fear caused me to follow any and all signs given to me about who I believed God said was my husband.

I had a dream of a description of a man who was presented as a friend, but I believed he was much more. Unfortunately, I made the mistake of trying to take matters into my own hands by putting a face and name to the mystery man presented to me in a dream. Trying to bring my dream to life led me into confusion, setback, and delay. In the dream, I saw a 6'2-6'3, dark, and built-ish looking man. At the time I was against the dream because dark and handsome wasn't my type. I was more into mocha chocolate or cappuccino complexed men. I found myself afraid of making a mistake so I decided to move based solely on the dream I had. Don't get me wrong, there have been people who dream of a man and years later they marry them, but there are also individuals who find themselves chasing shadows and receiving heartbreak. I can say I don't want to be on the heartbreak end of the spectrum. I believed I had found this mystery man, after all the former deceptions I faced, but he ended up not being at all what I expected. I use to believe in soul mates, that God who knows your beginning and end, would also design a partner who would be in your life to help your purpose and not destroy it. Now, I am more on the side of finding a guy you love, and that loves you back, and asking God if he and I are compatible. I've learned that just because someone loves you, doesn't mean they are compatible with you.

Love is a lot of things; *patient, kind, it doesn't boast and is not proud* (1Cor. 13:4-8), but to go into a marriage you need to also have passion, friendship, God, responsibility, endurance and the desire to cherish each other. I see why God showed me a man that was my friend because growing up I never valued friendships at the start of my relationship. I dated guys because I was attracted to them, and not because I fell in love with having their friendship in my life. Now, I need more than just an attraction to be in a lasting relationship, even marriage. If I end up marrying a guy who fits the description of the one in the dream, awesome. I will feel confident knowing that God's plan came to fruition in my life. Even if I don't marry the guy from the dream, I have learned in this journey to put aside my emotions because you do not want to get into any relationship based on your emotions. Why? Because emotions and feelings constantly change. It is an endurance race, not an emotional one. I advise leaving everything to God because his promises do come to pass, you don't have to make them come to pass. Don't live in fear of making a mistake, or don't set limitations on yourself by rejecting others for the "un-known." One thing I have learned from all this is I hate confusion

As time passed on, I opened myself back up for love. In July of 2021, I met a very open, sweet, and honest guy, and he showed me that there are still men in the world who believe in being open and straightforward. It felt good to be wanted and pursued, but we very quickly re-alized that we live very opposite lives from each other. It's funny how you can meet a person for the first time but get along as if you've known them for years. Many would say, "That's love at first sight." It's no secret that I'm keeping myself until marriage, and it's no secret that he is not. We both want to succeed and be great in the world, but in different ways. The question I had to ask myself was, "Would I be happy living in his world?"

No one is perfect. For instance, the bible is filled with imperfect people who God still used and loved, but at least they tried to be better and do better. I never try to change anyone to be who I want them to be because I don't believe in people changing people, that's the job of the Holy Spirit. All people can do is tell others the truth and inspire them through their actions and way of liv-ing. A guy who is honest, but lives freely and does what-ever he wants is scary to me because nothing is stopping him from doing whatever he wants in his relationship, marriage, etc. Honesty in a man and woman is great be-cause it builds trust in a relationship, but honesty does not mean that he/she won't hurt you or let go of bad hab-its that are displeasing to you. When someone shows you who they are, believe them.

When I was younger, I would see girls in relationships with guys who told them upfront that they were not looking for something serious. The girl knowing this would still stick around, maybe hoping he will fall in love and change. After years of staying and going through heartbreak, scandals, and pain, the two finally marry and within a few months divorce. Why is it that a woman can accept a man's flaws in their relationship, but then reject those flaws in their marriage? Whatever the reason is, I don't want that to be my story. I will listen when someone tells me who they are, and I will not hope to change them or make them into who I want them to be. Who and or what you are looking for is out there looking for you. I hope you receive better than you can ever imagine. The best is yet to come, never settle!

Chapter 5

The Friend(ship) of Life

I tried for many years to fit in with a certain group of people (what one may refer to as the "cool kids"), but for the past few years, I felt like I didn't belong. I didn't always feel this way, these groups of people I am referring to were once my friends; but as time passed and years went by, I began to feel a disconnect. At that point in my life I didn't understand why, I just began feeling isolated and outcasted. Things I once did and considered fun, I did not enjoy anymore. Hanging out with friends who still enjoyed certain activities was hard for me. I felt like I was forcing myself to be what I was not. I believe this was the beginning of what I call my "transformation phase", where God began transforming my life, so that I could begin moving into my purpose. My friends never pushed me away or excluded me from things, but something in me just never felt right.

God took me through this period of isolation in my life because he wanted to teach me how to understand people. One might ask, "How can isolation teach you how to understand people?" When I went through my phase of isolation, I began to understand people who were in the same situation. I knew how it felt to be popular, the most liked, and accepted, now I was in a position where all that was gone. I struggled with myself because even though I did not fit into a specific group anymore, I still wanted to. I did not understand the change that was taking place in my life, so I struggled with who I was becoming, and who I wanted to be. There would be many occasions where many of my friends would invite me out, or ask me why I was sitting by myself, and I did not have the answer. Maybe it was all the insecurities I had stopping me from feeling like I was good enough. However, one thing is for sure, through this phase in my life, I am able to understand why people push people away, and choose to be alone.

People like to call it being shy, or introverted, but there is a fear of being rejected that one plays over and over in their head, which causes them to withdraw. You can't be hurt or rejected by people if you stay away from them. I realize now that God wanted me to go through this phase, so that I can learn how it was to be popular, lonely, insecure, confident, outcasted, and accepted, so I can help those who struggle within themselves. Yes, I went through so much pain because of the loneliness, the feeling of rejection, and heartbreak, but if all that means that one day I can help someone who may be facing what I faced, then it was all worth it. One thing I learned is that the key to becoming who you want to be is believing that you are truly great. Get out of your head, and stop thinking about things that do not matter; "Will they like me, am I pretty enough, will they think I'm cool?" You don't need anyone to validate you or confirm who God already said you are. You are great because God created you great. You may not see it now but trust me all the great things about you that are hidden, will surely come to light. Don't believe the lies that jealous people have said about you. Find like-minded people, who share your same goals and beliefs because those people are the friends that will last a lifetime.

I can admit I have struggled lately with being a good friend. It seems that the more time and years I spent alone, caused me to become more distant. It's not that I don't show up for my friends when they need me to, or I don't advise them when they are confused or lost, but I have found comfort in being at home by myself. Many people have their definition of what a good friend is, and to many, I am a good friend, so why don't I feel that way? Is it that I feel guilty that I'd rather be at home watching movies and spending time with God, than going out to clubs? I don't believe the issue was whether or not I was a good friend, but that I did not have friends who shared the same views and values as me.

I was watching the Kevin Hart documentary recently, and Kevin said: "You can't choose the family you are born into, but friends are the family you choose." I realized I was never a bad friend — I just needed to surround myself with friends that had similar goals, beliefs, and visions as me. I believe the issue we have as people are, we don't know when to let go. The friends I met in college shared the same goals and interests as me at that time, and that was to pass and graduate. We related to the same issues and boy problems, but now that we are older and have grown, our goals and interest changed. Of course, these were my friends, so I held on to the friendship, but I later found myself surrounded by people who had different viewpoints and beliefs than me. In continuing a friendship with people who were no longer supposed to be in my inner circle, I began to feel as if I did not fit in. I started behaving as someone I was not, I questioned myself about who I was and wondered if I was wasting my time on my dreams and visions. I came to the conclusion that God's purpose for me, and his purpose for them, was not going to be achieved through our friendship. It was time to let go and move on.

The friends who surround you, and that you have chosen to be your "family", should love you, speak good about you, uplift you, tell you the truth even if it hurts, want the best for you, and share the same goals and interests as you. This does not mean that if you are going to school to be a lawyer, all your friends should be lawyers too. What it means to share the same goals and interests, is that you and your friends want the best for each other, you want to both be the best you can be in whatever field that may be in, and you both encourage each other to be great. I used to have friends that when I would say I want to become a millionaire one day, or I want to speak all over the world, they would discourage me and make me feel as if it was impossible and would never happen. It was not their fault, my dreams were not theirs. The more

I would hang around them, especially when things got tough, I would feel that they were right. The truth of the matter is, they were wrong. When I started hanging out with people who believed it possible to become a millionaire and achieve the impossible, I became more inspired and motivated to keep pushing for my dreams. The wrong friends can delay and hinder your purpose if you let them. There is a saying by John Minsheu, "Birds of a feather flock together." If you find yourself surrounded by friends who gossip, friends who don't believe in hard work, or friends who love fighting and causing hurt to others, it means either you too are like them, or you need to find a better set of friends. I just recently had to distance myself from one of my longtime friends because I found out that I was the headline of all her jokes. She would talk about me to her other friends, laugh at my former status and situation, and was speaking blasphemy against me.

I realized that being a good friend for me wasn't the issue; the issue was I was not aligning myself with like-minded people. One thing I have learned is that keeping yourself isolated is never the answer because isolation just brings loneliness. The best thing to do is take time to know yourself, figure out who you want to be, the things you love about yourself, and the things you don't. In doing this, you will figure out how to improve your strong areas, strengthen your weak areas, and surround yourself with friends who align with who you want to be. Gayle King and Oprah Winfrey have been friends for many years, have helped people in different ways, and have both achieved great things in the world today. Oprah and Gayle have a great friendship because they share common goals, and that goal is to help the world in whatever way they can. Friendships are not by force but by choice, so choose the best friends for yourself, and be the best friend for them as well!

Chapter 6

Knowing Who You Are

Life has a funny way of bringing up forgotten dreams, and making them your reality. As children, we have many plans of who we want to become — some want to become T.V. stars, while others want to become doctors. However, what if life hits you with the opposite, and you become the one thing you tried to run from. Being a woman of God I believe that God puts in us gifts that the enemy at a young age tries to destroy. For example, who would have thought in a million years that I would become a writer. Growing up, I hated writing although it was the only subject I received the highest-grade in. The irony, I know. I ran from writing my whole life, and writing became the one thing that gave me a purpose. It first showed in my poetry, which later turned to music, and now, years later, books. No one can ever predict how life will turn out for them, but one thing I do know is to always stay hopeful. Life may not be what you expected it to be, but if you just let it take its course, you will be amazed by the outcome. I recently watched Oprah's *2020 Vision Tour* in Dallas, Texas, with guest speaker Tracie Ellis Ross. Tracie Spoke about her fears of singing because she worried she would be compared to her mother, the award-winning singer, Diana Ross. This fear kept Tracie from pursuing her dreams of one day becoming a singer. As Tracie went more into details about this matter, I became more intrigued. I have followed Tracie's career from her hit TV show *Girlfriends* to now *Blackish*, and I never thought that her dream was to become a singer. I saw how great and funny she was in front of the cameras, and I assumed that she was living out her dream.

Growing up, I always wanted to have a voice of my own. I knew early on that singing was not my strength, so I later found my strength through rap music and writing. Although I had a lot of fears about my image, what I feared the most was having a gift that would never be used. As Tracie Ellis Ross was speaking to Oprah, I found myself asking the question, "How can someone be so gifted, but never use such a gift in life?" As I continued to listen to Oprah and Tracie's conversation, it all started to make sense. Although Tracie has a voice for singing, her purpose in life was much more. She was able to touch the lives of so many people by breaking the norms through her comedies, television shows, and Ted Talks. This was her purpose and the plan I believe God had for her life. The great thing about God is nothing is ever wasted. Now, fast-forward into 2020, Tracie Ellis Ross was given a movie role in which she will be playing a singer. Her talent and gift of singing are now aligning with her purpose. I believe that every talent God places in us has its time and purpose. I was able to learn through watching this Vision Tour with guest speaker Tracie Ellis Ross, that although we may have our fears, the gifts God has given us will never be wasted. I don't know if I will ever become a rapper, or how it relates to the plans God has for my life, but one thing I do know, my purpose is to speak to the world in one form or the other. It may be through music, blogging, writing books, creating a podcast, or all of the above. All I know is that when it is your time, your gifts and talents will shine.

Knowing what your gifts and talents are is important because it is what will lead you to your purpose. As a writer, I am able to view the world in different aspects. For example, I started as a rapper, and I believed that my music (compared to other artists), was great. Some would agree, that yes, I have a talent in that area, but is it my purpose? Suppose I make it as a rapper, I would have to promote, sell, attract, and connect. That means being where the hype is, and conforming to that lifestyle, and that's not me. I'm not much of a partygoer, I'm more of a laid-back "travel type". I asked the Holy Spirit, "What is my purpose?" It all then became clear to me: writing was my purpose. I was looking for my purpose in life, all awhile it was right in front of me. The music, blogging, speaking in public, all lead back to writing. I don't know what life has in store for me, but one thing I do know is the future looks bright. As Pastor T.D. Jakes once said, "I'll rather shoot high for something and fail, than not try shooting at all." Remember, your future depends on the decisions you make.

For many people, especially those who have a strict cultural background, who they are comes from their status, titles, and success. When a child or person does not achieve such success, they tend to look down on such a person, because they did not meet the status-quo of what they deemed success to be. To others, success is how much money you make, in the words of Drake, "What's your net worth?" Having nice cars, designer clothes, and glamorous things all around you means you are someone of importance. So what would you call a person who has neither riches nor a degree? Throughout my life, I had an urge for greatness, I desired to make a great amount of wealth, and reach levels in life no one else in my family has reached. My reasons for reaching such heights had no mere purpose only to show off, so that people could see all I had and envy me. When I started focusing more on God, I stopped caring about reaching the success everybody else wanted for me, but instead reaching the success I wanted for myself. The only issue was I did not truly understand what success was to me, so how was I going to reach it. My confusion led me into a big depression. I felt at a certain point as if I was a loser, because I was neither rich, a doctor, nor a nurse. I began to fill my voids of failure by looking at men who had what I lacked. Even though I was not aware of it at the time, I was attracted to men that were great in an area of their life. If I would see a guy who had popularity, fame, riches, or a big title like a doctor, or football player, I would become interested. The truth was I saw in him levels of greatness that I always wanted but was not achieving at the time, so I wanted to be a part of theirs. When I got closer to God and started building a personal relationship with him, was when I started understanding what success truly is. We are taught that success is what you achieve, but it is more than that. We all have a purpose in life, and that purpose is what leads us to our destiny. Until you achieve that, you have not been successful in life. I had to search deep within myself with the help of the Holy Spirit to find out what my purpose was. I don't want to live in the shadows of a man or live in the expectations of people. I want the plans I have for myself to be in accordance with the plans God has for me, so that my greatness can show forth and I can achieve great success.

As you grow in life, certain gifts and talents (some call them skills), will begin to manifest. God gives different talents and skills to every person, but that does not mean that talent is what will lead you into your purpose. For example, when I turned 14 years old I started doing hair and I believe God gave me that talent, not because he wanted me to open a salon and become a hairstylist, but because that season required me to pick up a skill that will help make things easier for my family. Growing up my parents had financial difficulties, so at a point in time it became difficult for me and my sisters to go to the salon and get our hair done, so we had to learn and help ourselves. From learning to do my own hair, I was able to grow and began doing other peoples' hair as well. This was a talent I needed at this time, because it not only helped save money for my family, but it also gave me a source of income that I used to pay for prom and other personal things. My family and I were in a season of need, and God gave me the talent to survive it. What I am trying to say is don't look at your talents as a career path, but as a way of help. Why people get stuck in life is because they are good at doing many things and become confused about what their exact purpose is. When trying to find the purpose God has planned for your life, you must gain a deeper understanding and connection to the Holy Spirit, so that the spirit of God can reveal to you the way you should go.

It is said that people are a product of their environment and that where and how an individual grows up can determine how their life will end up. I had a discussion previously with someone who was born in Nigeria. This person believed that American-born Nigerians do not take advantage of all the opportunities America has to offer. I had to agree to disagree. It is true that people that come from other countries see all that they can be and achieve here in America, so they work harder to reach their dreams, whereas many individuals born here are just trying to live or get by. I believe that the same way a Nigerian born can come to America, see all it has to offer, and succeed, is the same way an American born can go to Nigeria, see all it has to offer, and succeed. A Nigerian can travel to a new environment and capitalize from it, in the same way Americans can go to Africa and capitalize on gold, oil, etc. So the question is, Why do people struggle to succeed in countries where they are born?

I asked a guy born in Nigeria this same question, and he said, "People are a product of their mindset, not a country." If you are a lazy person, even if you move to Europe, you'll still be a lazy person, until the mindset of "I don't want to do anything" is broken. Can an environment do that? Yes, it can. If you are in an environment where everyone has to walk to get to where they are going, you won't have a choice but to walk. Just like if you are around hard-working people, who push you every day, their habits can rub off on you, causing you to change also. Although I agree with this theory, I also believe that a lazy person can still decide to drive, even if that means going to work late or being stuck in traffic. As people, we can adapt to the surroundings we find ourselves in. Even with this trait of adaptability, how you think does determine how far you go. A person that believes nothing is impossible will push him or herself to work harder in achieving their goal. A person who believes they aren't good enough, or will never be accepted, holds themselves back from even trying. If you were to switch a businessman's position with that of a gatekeeper, guess what will happen. The businessman will still have the same business mindset, and unknowingly still build connections and see how to capitalize off the small he is given, while a gatekeeper will still have the mindset of small, and will not take the necessary risks needed to move the business forward. In other words, the business would likely collapse if the gatekeeper's mind does not change, and the businessman will still find a way to create a new business or connect with people for new ventures. To succeed and reach all the dreams and goals you have for yourself, you have to change your way of thinking. Are you thinking small, negatively, fearfully, and doubtfully, or are you thinking big, positively, hopeful, and expectant?

After the conversation ended, I realized that he is right about one thing. People have to stop making excuses about why they aren't where they are today. Many people have been in the same situation you are in today, but why did they succeed, and why haven't you? I hope everyone will believe that they too can succeed, and do all it takes to get to their destination. Remember all dreams can be achieved, with faith, hard work, consistency, and perseverance. When trying to understand if what you are doing or wanting to do is God's purpose for your life, ask yourself these questions:

1. Is what you're doing causing you to sin against God?
2. Are you doing it for the wrong reasons?
3. Can you touch lives in that area?
4. Do you have peace, and are you being your true self?

I hope after answering these questions you gained some clarity on what your purpose is in life. Even if after you've answered these questions you are still confused, remember life is a journey, and no one can say they have it 100% correct. In anything you do, you should have peace. I'm sure Oprah has her stories of how the pressures of life got to her, but she still had peace and fulfillment in what she is called to do because it is her purpose. Beyoncé might not want to go to rehearsal every single day, but she loves what she does, so that passion pushes her to go the extra mile. What I'm saying is, life can be exhausting at times, but when you are in alignment with your purpose, you will find joy even in the little things.

Let Us Pray

I pray that as you've read this book, you will find peace in knowing that everything will work out for your good. I pray that you will be in alignment with your purpose and destiny, and I pray that you will find true joy and happiness in all that you do. I pray that the storms of life will not overcome you, but pass you by, as you dwell in the shelter of God. I pray that true love, destined by God, will locate and find you, and I pray that you will be surrounded by friends who love and care for you. I pray that you continue in strength to persevere and never give up, and I pray that God in his Grace and Mercy will take all your pains away. May the peace of the Lord be with you, and may he always shine his face upon you. May all things go well with you, and may God turn all impossibilities in your life to possibilities in Jesus' name I pray.

Amen!